GUNS · N · ROSES

GREATEST HITS

Cherry Lane Music Company
Director of Publications/Project Editor: Mark Phillips

ISBN 978-1-60378-429-0

Visit our website at www.cherrylaneprint.com

Welcome to the Jungle

Words and Music by
W. Axl Rose, Slash,
Izzy Stradlin', Duff McKagan
and Steven Adler

Faster ♩ = 124

1. Wel-come to the jun - gle, we got fun 'n' games.___
2.3. *See additional lyrics*

We got ev - 'ry - thing_ you want,_ hon - ey, we know the names.__ We are the

I'm gon-na watch you bleed!

Bridge

And when you're high___

___ you nev - er   ev - er want to come down,___   so

7

down, ___ so down, ___ so down. _____

Yeah! _____

_____ Now!

You know where you are?   You're in the jun - gle, ba - by!

You're gon - na   die! _____

In the jun - gle.   Wel - come to the jun - gle. Watch it bring you to your

sha na na na na na na na na na na na knees, knees.__ In the jun-

gle. Wel-come to the jun - gle. Feel__ my, oh, my, my,__

my ser-pen-tine.__ Jun-gle. Wel-come to the jun - gle. Watch it bring you to your

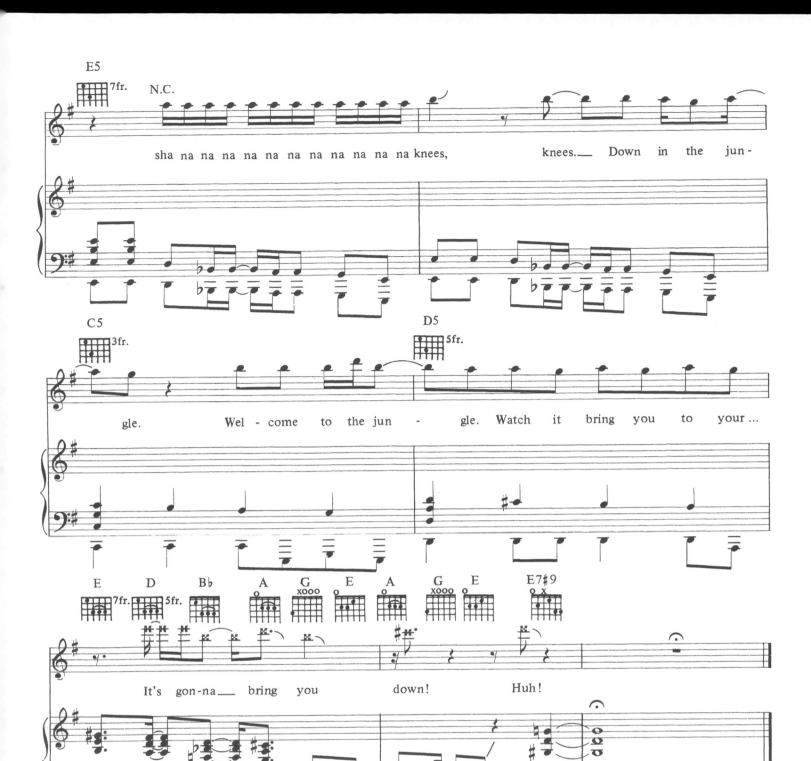

Additional Lyrics

2. Welcome to the jungle, we take it day by day.
If you want it, you're gonna bleed, but it's the price you pay.
And you're a very sexy girl who's very hard to please.
You can taste the bright lights, but you won't get them for free.
In the jungle. Welcome to the jungle.
Feel my, my, my serpentine.
I wanna hear you scream!

3. Welcome to the jungle, it gets worse here every day.
You learn to live like an animal in the jungle where we play.
If you got a hunger for what you see, you'll take it eventually,
You can have anything you want, but you better not take it from me.
In the jungle. Welcome to the jungle.
Watch it bring you to your sha na na na na na na na na na na na knees, knees.
I'm gonna watch you bleed! *(To Bridge)*

Sweet Child o' Mine

Words and Music by
W. Axl Rose, Slash,
Izzy Stradlin', Duff McKagan
and Steven Adler

1. She's got a smile___ that it seems to me___ re-minds___ me of child - hood
2. *See additional lyrics.*

mem - o - ries, ___ where ev - 'ry - thing___ was as fresh___

as the bright blue sky.

Now and then when I see her face she takes me a-way to that

spe - cial place, and if I stared too long. I'll

prob-'ly break down and cry.

Chorus

Whoa,   whoa,_ whoa,_ sweet child   o' mine._

Whoa,   oh,_ oh, oh,_   sweet love o' mine._

To Coda

D.S. al Coda

Additional Lyrics

2. She's got eyes of the bluest skies, as if they thought of rain.
   I hate to look into those eyes and see an ounce of pain.
   Her hair reminds me of a warm safe place where as a child I'd hide,
   And pray for the thunder and the rain to quietly pass me by. *(To Chorus)*

Patience

Words and Music by
W. Axl Rose, Slash,
Izzy Stradlin', Duff McKagan
and Steven Adler

There is no doubt__ you're in__ my heart__ now.

Said, wom-an,__ take it slow,__ it-'ll

work it-self__ out fine.__ All we need__ is

just a lit-tle pa-tience.

Said, sug - ar,___ make it slow___ and we come to - geth - er fine.___

All we need___ is just___ a lit - tle pa -

tience.

1.

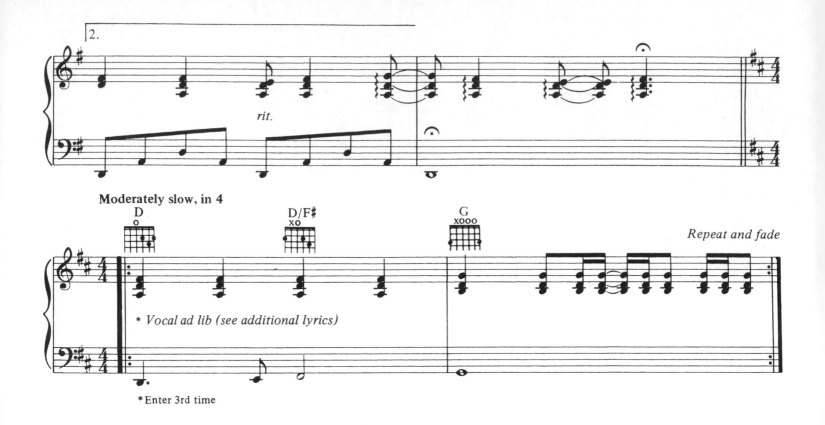

Moderately slow, in 4

Repeat and fade

* *Vocal ad lib (see additional lyrics)*

*Enter 3rd time

Additional Lyrics

2. I sit here on the stairs 'cause I'd rather be alone.
   If I can't have you right now I'll wait, dear.
   Sometimes I get so tense but I can't speed up the time.
   But you know, love, there's one more thing to consider.

   Said, woman, take it slow and things will be just fine.
   You and I'll just use a little patience.
   Said, sugar, take the time 'cause the lights are shining bright.
   You and I've got what it takes to make it.
   We won't fake it, ah, I'll never break it 'cause I can't take it.

Vocal ad lib:

   Little patience, mm, yeah, mm, yeah.
   Need a little patience, yeah.
   Just a little patience, yeah.
   Some more patience.
   I been walkin' the streets at night
   Just tryin' to get it right.
   Hard to see with so many around.
   You know I don't like being stuck in the ground,
   And the streets don't change, but baby the name.
   I ain't got time for the game 'cause I need you.
   Yeah, yeah, but I need you, oo, I need you.
   Woh, I need you, oo, this time.

Paradise City

Words and Music by
W. Axl Rose, Slash,
Izzy Stradlin', Duff McKagan
and Steven Adler

Take me down_ to the par - a - dise ci - ty, where the grass is green and the girls are pret - ty.

Oh, won't you please take me home. _____

1. Just a ur-chin liv-in' un-der the street. I'm a ____ hard case thats tough to beat. ____ I'm your
2.3.4. *See additional lyrics*

char - i -ty case, ___ so buy me some-thing to eat. ___ I'll pay you at an-oth-er time.

1.
N.C.
Take it to the end of the line. ___

2.
N.C.
Ev-'ry-bod-y's do-in' their time. ___

Chorus

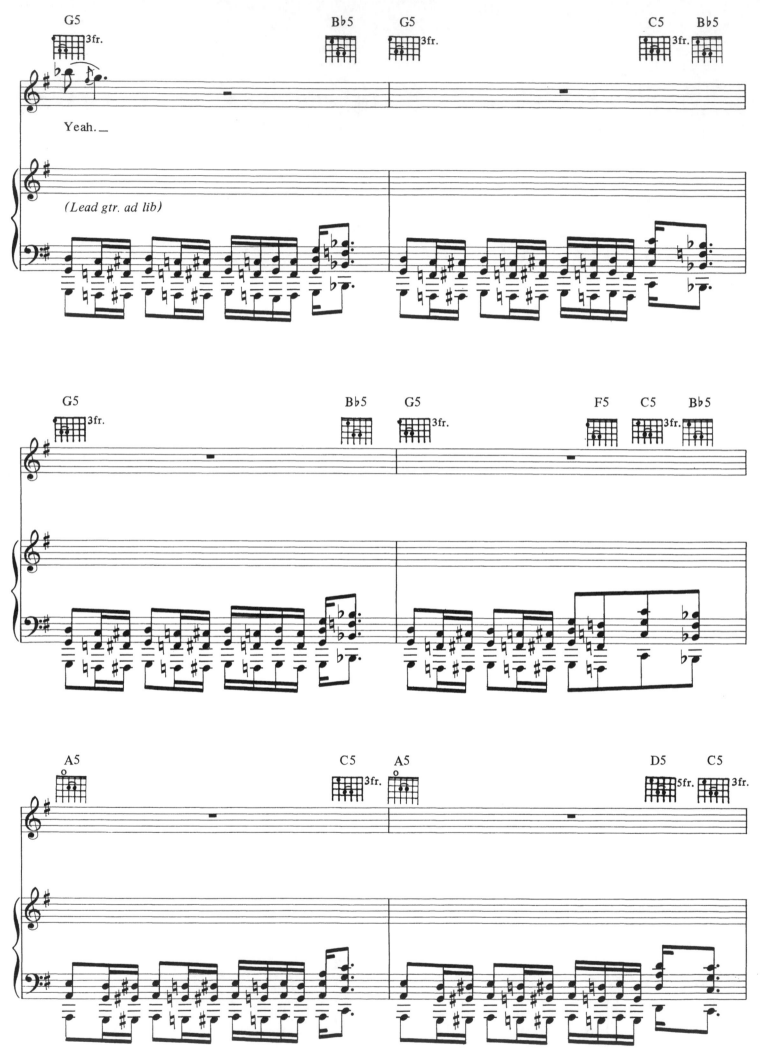

Yeah. _

(Lead gtr. ad lib)

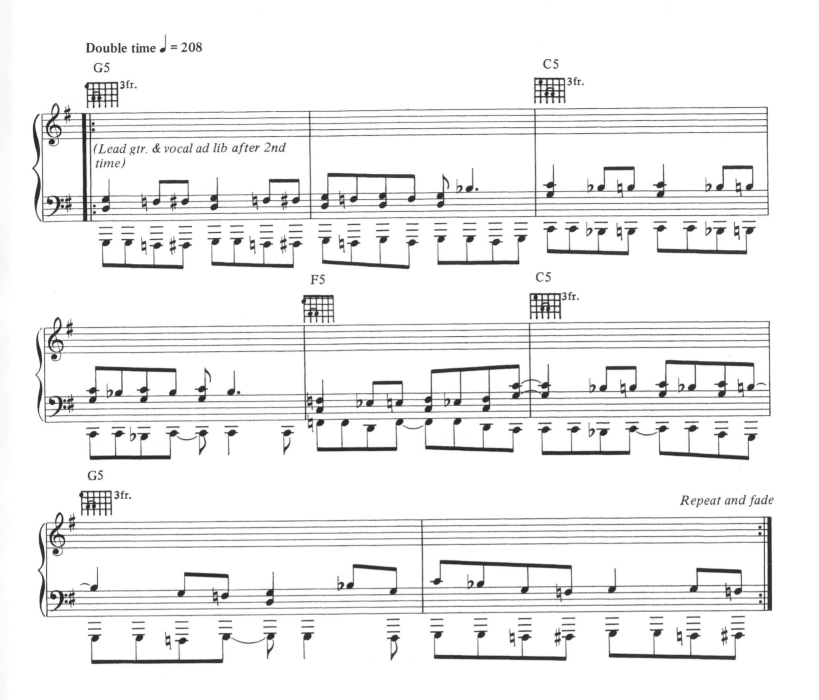

Additional Lyrics

2. Ragz to richez, or so they say.
   Ya gotta keep pushin' for the fortune and fame.
   It's all a gamble when it's just a game.
   Ya treat it like a capital crime.
   Everybody's doin' their time. *(To Chorus)*

3. Strapped in the chair of the city's gas chamber,
   Why I'm here I can't quite remember.
   The surgeon general says it's hazarous to breathe.
   I'd have anothe cigarette but I can't see.
   Tell me who ya gonna believe? *(To Chorus)*

4. Captain America's been torn a part.
   Now he's a court jester with a broken heart.
   He said, "Turn me around and take me back to the start."
   I must be losin' my mind. "Are you blind?"
   I've seen it all a million times. *(To Chorus)*

Knockin' on Heaven's Door

Words and Music by
Bob Dylan

Ma - ma, take this badge from me.
Ma - ma, put my guns in the ground.

I can't use it an - y - more.
I can't shoot them an - y - more.

* Recorded a half step lower.

Knock, knock, knock-in' on heav-en's door.____

Knock, knock, knock-in' on heav-en's door.____

Civil War

Words and Music by
Slash, Duff McKagan
and W. Axl Rose

Moderately slow

mp

Look at your young men fight - ing.
Look at the hate we're breed - ing.

Look at your wom - en cry - ing.
Look at the fear we're feed - ing.

Look at your young men dy - ing, the way they've al - ways done be - fore.
Look at the lives we're lead - ing, the way we've al - ways done be - fore.

* Recorded a half step lower.

never fell— for Vi-et-nam,— we got the wall of D. C.— to re-mind us all— that you

can't trust free-dom when it's not in your hands,— when ev-'ry-bod-y's fight-in' for their prom-ised land,— and

cresc.

Chorus

I don't need— your civ-il war.—

f

It feeds the rich— while it bur-ies the poor.—

40

You Could Be Mine

Words and Music by
Izzy Stradlin' and W. Axl Rose

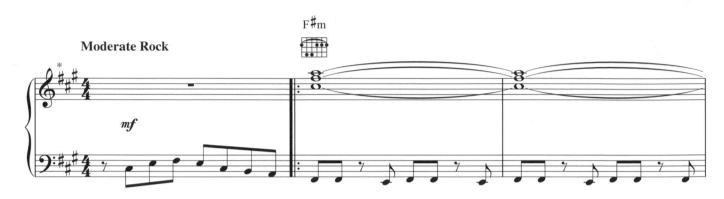

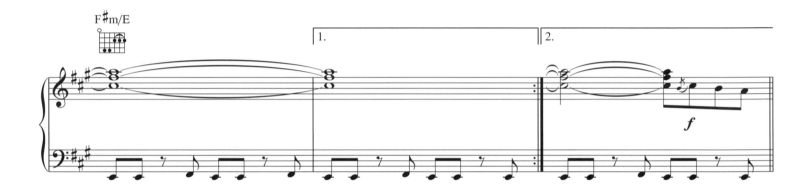

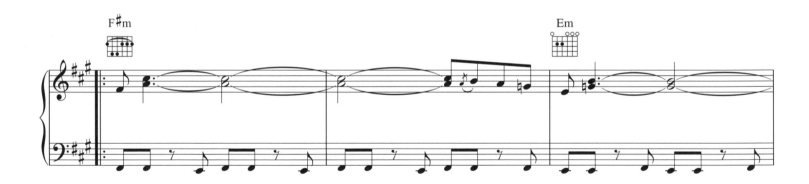

*Recorded a half step lower.

I'm a cold heart-break-er, fit to burn,_ and I'll rip your heart in two_ and I'll leave you ly-in' on the bed._ Well, I'll be out the door_ be-

fore you wake; _ it's noth- in' new to you ____ 'cause I

think we've seen that mov - ie, too. _____

'Cause you could be

mine, ____ but you're way

out of line. _____ With your

bitch slap rap - pin' and your co - caine tongue, _ you get noth - in'

To Codas I & II

done. I said, you could be

mine. _____

ry.   When I come home late at night, don't

ask me where I've been.   Just count your

stars I'm home a - gain.   'Cause

D.S. al Coda I

Coda I

you   could be   mine.

You could be mine.

You could be mine.

49

must you find ___

an - oth - er rea - son to cry? ___ *(Sing 1st time only)*

1.

2.

B5

While you're break - in' down my back and I been

C#5

rack - in' out __ my brain, __ it don't mat - ter how we make it 'cause it al -

C#5   B5

ways ends the same. __ You can push it for more mile - age but your

C#5   D5

flaps are wear - ing thin. And I __ could sleep on it till morn - ing but this

Ow!   You could be   mine. _____   You could be   mine. _

Oh, _____   you could be   mine. _____

I   know   you could be   mine. _____   Oh, _____   you could be   mine. _

Freely
Tacet

_____   You could be   mine. _____   Yeah.

Don't Cry
(Original)

Words and Music by
Izzy Stradlin' and W. Axl Rose

* Recorded a half step lower.

There's a heav-en a-bove you, ba - by. And don't you cry.

Don't you ev - er cry. Don't you cry to-night.

Ba - by, may - be some day. And don't you cry.

Don't you ev - er cry. Don't you cry to-night.

Freely

November Rain

Words and Music by
W. Axl Rose

* Recorded a half step lower

When I look in-to your eyes, I can see a love re-strained.

But dar-lin', when I hold you, don't you know I feel the same?

you, don't you know I feel the same?

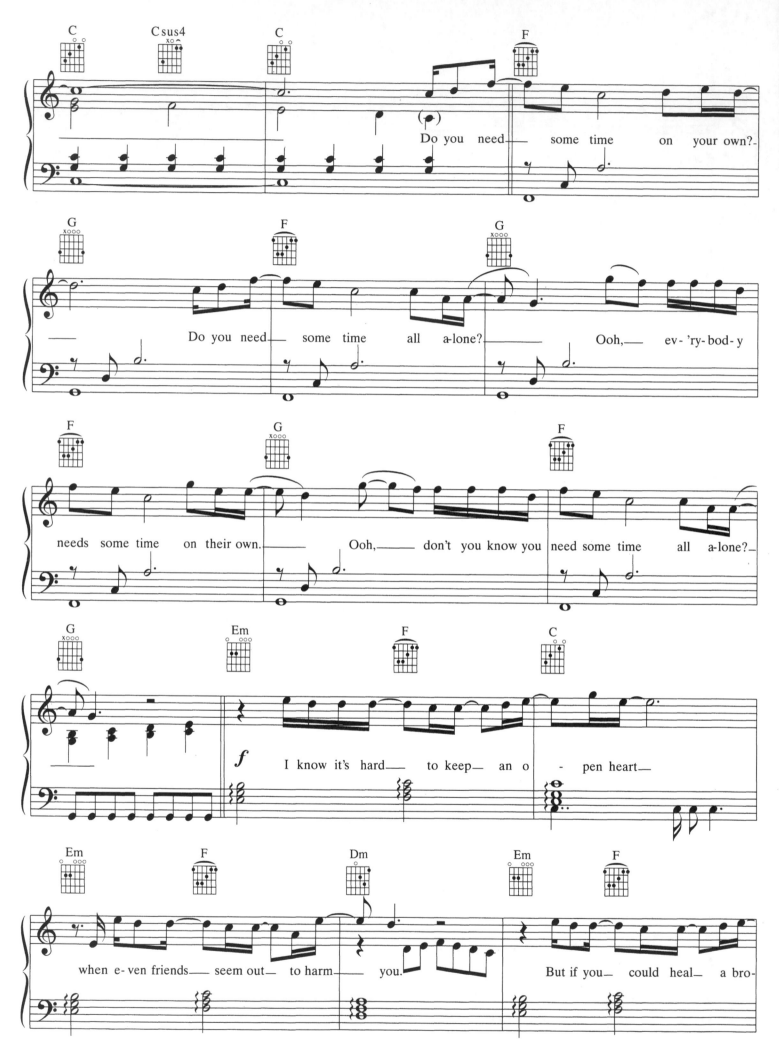

Do you need some time on your own?

Do you need some time all a-lone? Ooh, ev-'ry-bod-y

needs some time on their own. Ooh, don't you know you need some time all a-lone?

I know it's hard to keep an o - pen heart

when e-ven friends seem out to harm you. But if you could heal a bro-

ken heart,— would-n't time— be out— to charm— you? Woh.—

Some-times I need some time on my own. Some-times I

need some time all a-lone. Ooh, ev-'ry-bod-y needs some time on their own.

Ooh, don't you know you need some time all a-lone?

And when your fears____ sub-side____

____ and shad-ows still____ re-main,____

I know that you____ can love me when there's no one left to blame.

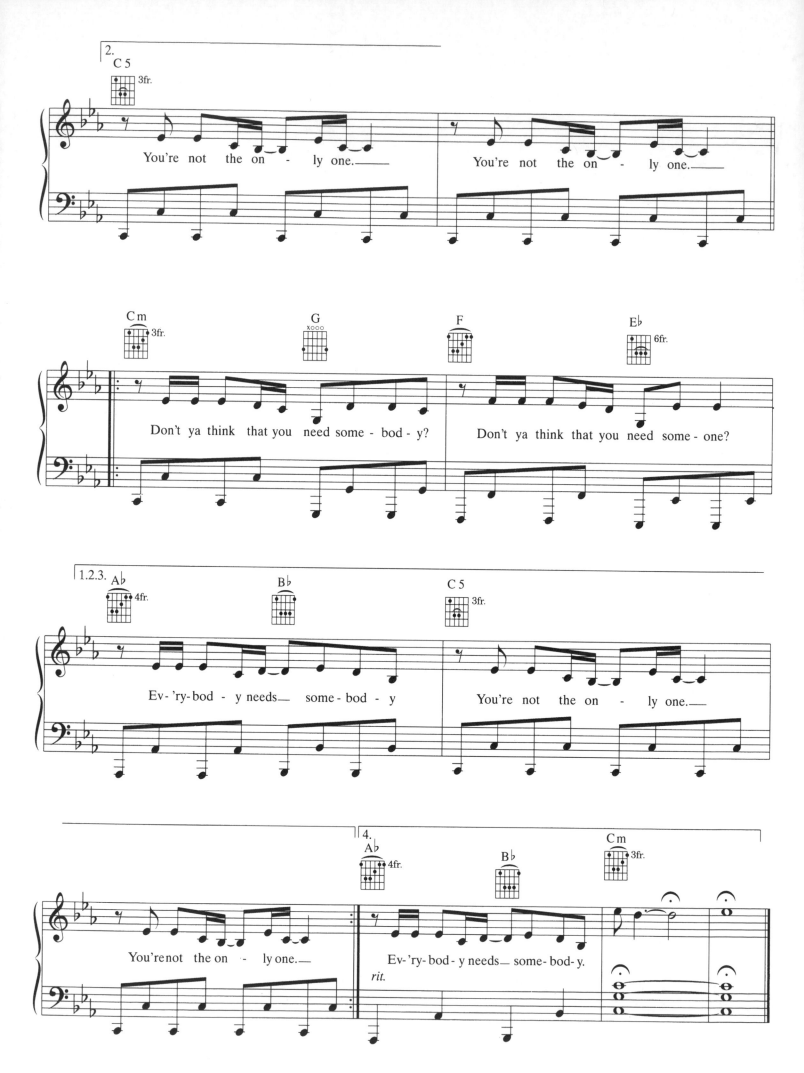

Live and Let Die

Words and Music by
Paul McCartney and Linda McCartney

* Recorded a half step lower.

A little faster

die,_____ live and let die._____

Uptempo Rock

Half time, Raggae feel

Pianists: Omit vocal melody next 5 bars.

What does it mat - ter to— ya? When you got a job to do— ya got to do it well.— You got to give the oth - er fel - la hell.—

Yesterdays

Words and Music by
W. Axl Rose, West Arkeen,
Billy McCloud and Del James

Moderately slow Rock

1. Yes- ter- day_____ there was so man- y things__ I was nev- er told.__
2.3. *See additional lyrics*

Now that I'm start- in' to learn,__ I feel I'm grow- in' old.__ 'Cause

yes- ter- day's__ got noth- in' for me.__ Old pic- tures that I'll al- ways see.__

* Recorded a half step lower.

Additional Lyrics

2. Prayers in my pocket
   And no hand in destiny.
   I'll keep on movin' along
   With no time to plant my feet.
   'Cause yesterday's got nothin' for me.
   Old pictures that I'll always see.
   Some things could be better
   If we'd all just let them be. *(To Chorus)*

3. Yesterday there were so many things
   I was never shown.
   Suddenly this time I found
   I'm on the streets and I'm all alone.
   Yesterday's got nothin' for me.
   Old pictures that I'll always see.
   I ain't got time to reminisce
   Old novelties. *(To Chorus)*

Ain't It Fun

Words and Music by
Cheetah Chrome and Peter Laughner

*Recorded a half step lower.

B5   D5   A

Ain't it fun when you   tell her   she's just a...

G   B5

And ain't it fun when she

D5   A   G   B5

splits and   leaves _ you on the   bum? _

G   B5   G

Well, ain't it fun when you've   bro-ken up   ev-'ry band __ that you ev-er be-gun? _

90

fun.   Such   fun.

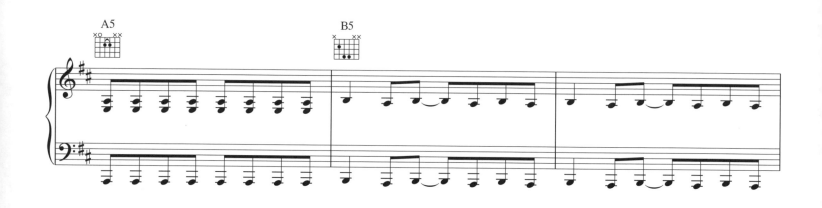

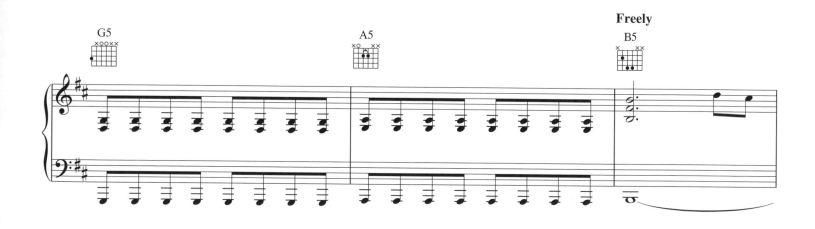

Freely

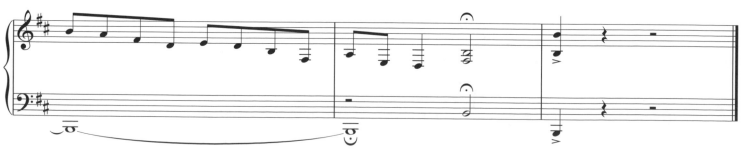

Since I Don't Have You

Words and Music by James Beaumont,
Janet Vogel, Joseph Verscharen, Walter Lester,
Lennie Martin, Joseph Rock and John Taylor

Moderately slow, in 4

*Recorded a half step lower.

Ooh. _____

D.S. al Coda

since   I don't   have   you. _____   Oh. _____

You, ___   you, ___   you, ___ oh, oh, _____ oh. _____

oh, _____   yeah.

Repeat and fade

98

Sympathy for the Devil

Words and Music by
Mick Jagger and Keith Richards

Moderate Rock

Please al-low me to in-tro-duce my-self; I'm a

*Vocal doubled by spoken lyric till Chorus.

man of wealth and taste. I've been a-round for a long,

long year, stole man-y a man's soul and

*Recorded a half step lower.

faith.   I was a-round __ when Je - sus __ Christ __ had his

mo - ment   of   doubt   and   pain.

Made __ damn __ sure __ Pi - late   washed __ his

hands   and sealed his   fate.   Oh!

B
Pleased to meet you; hope you guess my name.
E
Oh, yeah.
B
But what's puz-zlin' you is the
na-ture of my
E
game.
E
I stuck a-round Saint
D
Pe-ters-burg when I

saw it was __ a time __ for a change. __

I killed the czar and his min - is - ters; __ An - a -

sta - sia screamed __ in vain.

I rode a tank, held a gen - 'ral's rank _____ when the

na - ture of __ my game. ___ Ha, ha!

I watched with glee as your kings __ and queens fought for
(Ooh, ooh. ___ Ooh, ooh. ___

ten dec - ades _____ for the gods they made. _____ I
Ooh, ooh. ___ Ooh, ooh. ___

shout - ed out, __ "Who killed __ the Ken - ne - dys?" When
Ooh, ooh. ___ Ooh, ooh. ___

killed be-fore ___ they reach ___ Bom - bay. ___
Ooh, ___ ooh. ___
Ooh, ___ ooh. ___

Ooh, ___ ooh.) ___
Pleased to meet ___ you;
(Ooh, ___ ooh. ___

hope you guess my ___ name. _____
Ooh, ___ ooh. ___
Ooh, ___ ooh. ___

yeah. ___
Ooh, ___ ooh. ___
But ___ what's puz - zlin' ___ you ___ is the
Ooh, ___ ooh. ___

107

Coda I

E

game. ___
Ooh,   ooh.) ___   Oh,   yeah.

E   D

Just as   ev - 'ry cop's a   crim - i - nal ___   and

A   E

all ___   the sin - ners   saints, ___   as heads is tails, just call me

D   A   E

Lu - ci - fer,   'cause I'm in need of   some ___ re - straint.   If you

More Great Piano/Vocal Books

FROM CHERRY LANE

For a complete listing of Cherry Lane titles available,
including contents listings, please visit our web site at
www.cherrylane.com

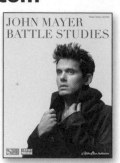